The Big Book Of
Acoustic Hits

Exclusive Distributors:
Music Sales Limited
8/9 Frith Street, London W1D 3JB, UK.

Order No. HLE90002803
ISBN 1-84609-365-1
This book © Copyright 2005 by Hal Leonard Europe

Cover design by Chloë Alexander
Printed in the USA

Your Guarantee of Quality
As publishers, we strive to produce every book to the highest commercial standards.
The book has been carefully designed to minimise awkward page turns and to make playing from it a real pleasure.
Throughout, the printing and binding have been planned to ensure a sturdy, attractive publication
which should give years of enjoyment.
If your copy fails to meet our high standards, please inform us and we will gladly replace it.

www.musicsales.com

This publication is not authorised for sale in the
United States of America and/or Canada.

Hal Leonard Europe
Distributed by Music Sales

ACROSS THE UNIVERSE

Words and Music by JOHN LENNON
and PAUL McCARTNEY

Words are flow-ing out __ like end-less rain __ in-to a pa-per cup, they slith-er while _ they pass, they slip a-way __ a-cross the u-ni-verse. __

Pools of sor-row, waves of joy are drift-ing through my o-pened mind, _ pos-

D.S. al Coda

AGAINST THE WIND

Words and Music by
BOB SEGER

noth - in' left ____ to burn ___ and noth - in' left to prove. ___
wor - ried a - bout pay - in', or e - ven how much I owed. ___

End instrumental

And I re - mem - ber what she ___ said to
Mov - in' eight miles a min - ute for months at a
Well, those drift - er's days are ____ past me

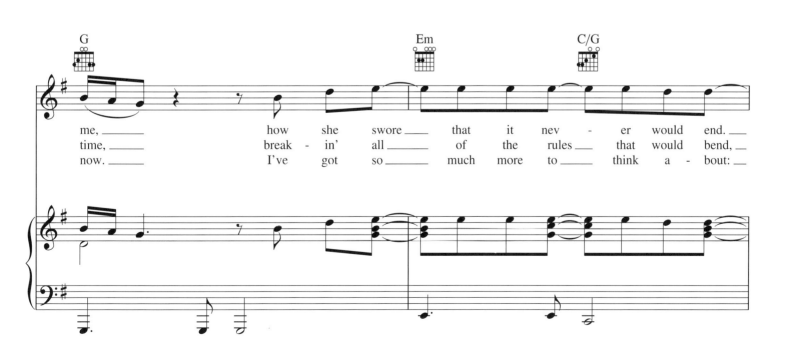

me, ____ how she swore ___ that it nev - er would end. ___
time, ____ break - in' all ___ of the rules ___ that would bend, __
now. ____ I've got so ___ much more to ___ think a - bout: __

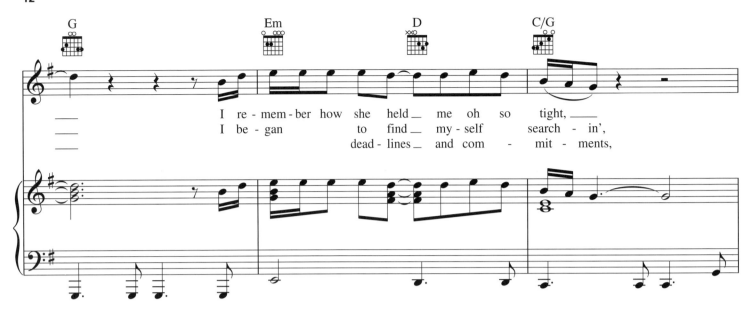

I re - mem - ber how she held __ me oh so tight, ____
I be - gan to find __ my - self search - in',
dead - lines __ and com - mit - ments,

Wish I did - n't know now what I did - n't know then.
search - in' for shel - ter a - gain and a - gain.
what to leave in, what to leave out.

A - gainst the wind, __
A - gainst the wind, __
A - gainst the wind, __

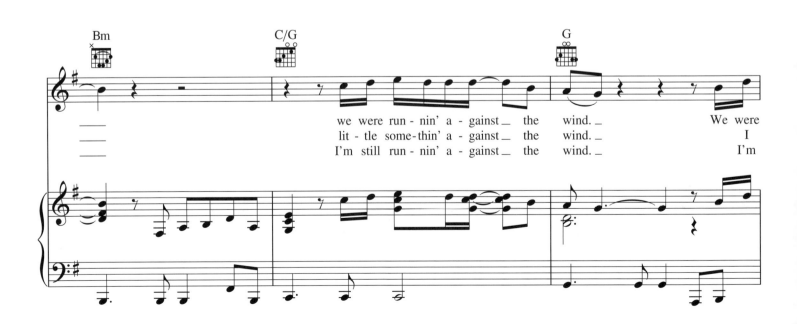

we were run - nin' a - gainst __ the wind. __ We were
lit - tle some - thin' a - gainst __ the wind. __ I
I'm still run - nin' a - gainst __ the wind. __ I'm

ALL FOR YOU

Words and Music by KEN BLOCK, JEFF BERES,
ANDREW COPELAND, RYAN NEWELL
and MARK TROJANOWSKI

a sound _____ com - ing from ___ your eyes. _____

D.S. al Coda

Fin - 'lly I fig -

CODA

hard   to   say ___ what   it   is ___ I   see ___ in   you. ___

ALL I HAVE TO DO IS DREAM

Words and Music by
BOUDLEAUX BRYANT

Moderately

Dream, _____ dream, dream, dream, _ Dream, _____ dream, dream, dream._ When

I want you in my arms, When I want you and all your charms When
I feel blue in the night, And I need you to hold me tight When

AMAZED

Words and Music by MARV GREEN,
CHRIS LINDSEY and AIMEE MAYO

Moderately slow Country Ballad

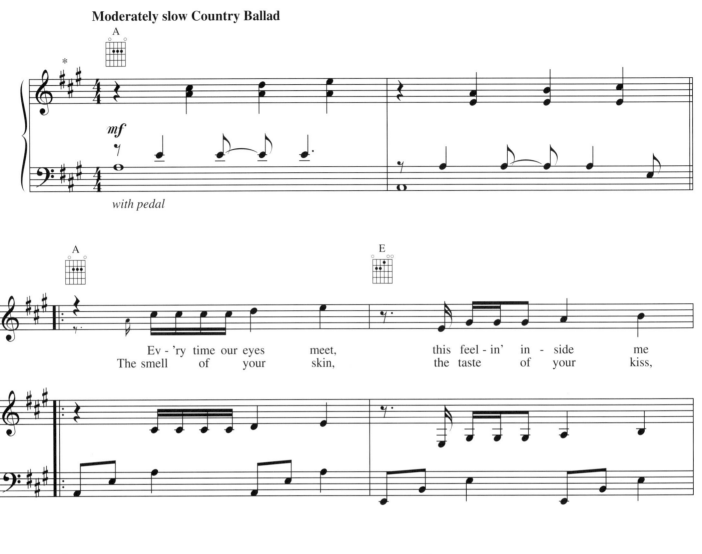

Ev - 'ry time our eyes meet, this feel - in' in - side me
The smell of your skin, the taste of your kiss,

is al - most more— than I—— can take.——
the way you whis - per in—— the dark.——

*Recorded a half step lower.

I wan-na spend the rest of my life____ with you by my side____ for-ev-er and_ ev - er.

Ev-'ry lit-tle thing that you do,__

oh,_____ ev-'ry lit-tle thing that you_ do,__

Freely

Tempo I

Tacet

____ ba-by, I'm a-mazed_ by__ you.

mp *rit.*

AMERICAN TUNE

Words and Music by
PAUL SIMON

AND I LOVE YOU SO

Words and Music by
DON McLEAN

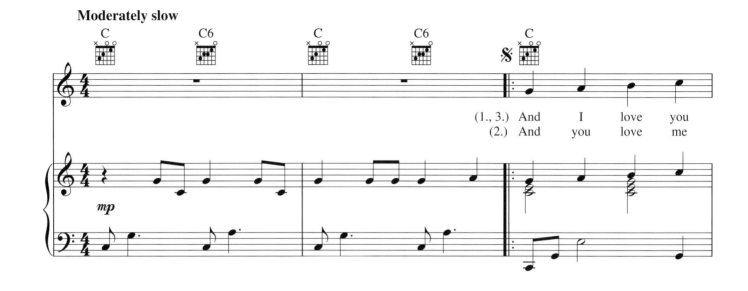

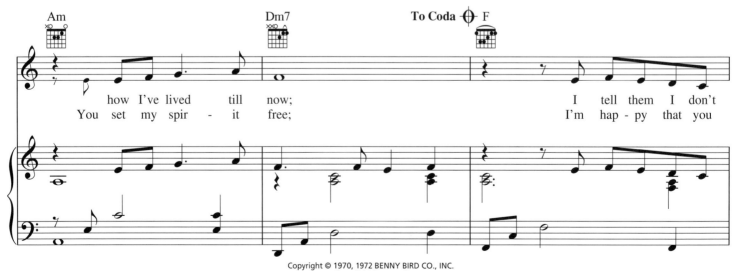

ANGIE

Words and Music by MICK JAGGER
and KEITH RICHARDS

44

BEHIND BLUE EYES

Words and Music by
PETE TOWNSHEND

No one knows___ what it's like _____ to be the bad ___ man,
No one knows___ what it's like _____ to feel these feel - ings

to be the sad ___ man _____ be - hind ___
like I do, _____ and I ___

___ blue eyes. ___
___ blame you. ___

No one knows___ what it's like ___
No one bites___ back as hard ___

BABE, I'M GONNA LEAVE YOU

Words and Music by ANNE BREDON,
JIMMY PAGE and ROBERT PLANT

sum - mer comes a - long. _____

Ba - ba, __ ba, __ ba, __ ba, __ ba, __ ba - by. Ba - by,

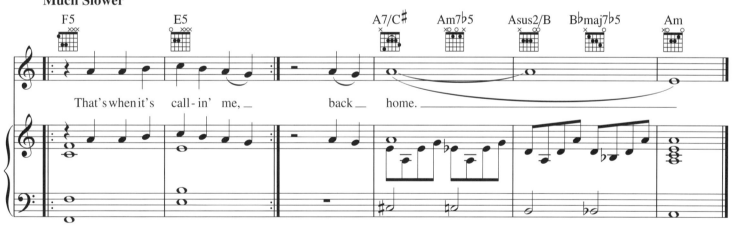

That's when it's call-in' me, ___ back ___ home. _____

Additional Lyrics

I know, I know, I know, I never, I never, I never, I never, I never leave you, baby
But I got to go away from this place, I've got to quit you.
Ooh, baby, baby, baby, baby
Baby, baby, baby, ooh don't you hear it callin'?
Woman, woman, I know, I know it's good to have you back again
And I know that one day, baby, it's really gonna grow, yes it is.
We gonna go walkin' through the park every day.
Hear what I say, every day.
Baby, it's really growin', you made me happy when skies were grey.
But now I've got to go away
Baby, baby, baby, baby
That's when it's callin' me
That's when it's callin' me back home...

BAND ON THE RUN

Words and Music by PAUL
and LINDA McCARTNEY

BE-BOP-A-LULA

Words and Music by TEX DAVIS
and GENE VINCENT

THE BOXER

Words and Music by
PAUL SIMON

BUILDING A MYSTERY

Words and Music by SARAH McLACHLAN
and PIERRE MARCHAND

CASTLES IN THE AIR

Words and Music by
DON McLEAN

BYE BYE LOVE

Words and Music by FELICE BRYANT
and BOUDLEAUX BRYANT

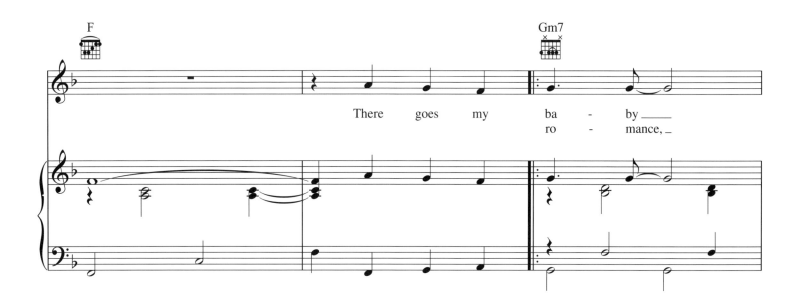

There goes my ba - by _____
ro - mance, _____

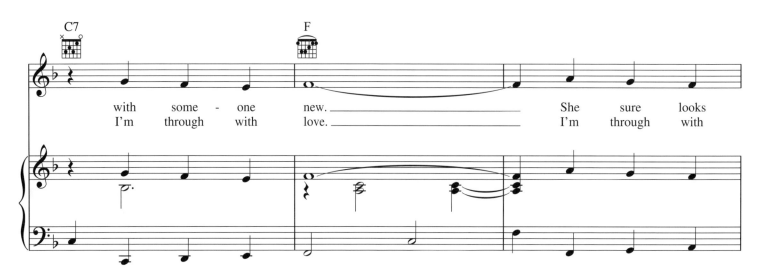

with   some - one   new. _____   She   sure   looks
I'm   through   with   love. _____   I'm   through   with

CHAMPAGNE SUPERNOVA

Words and Music by
NOEL GALLAGHER

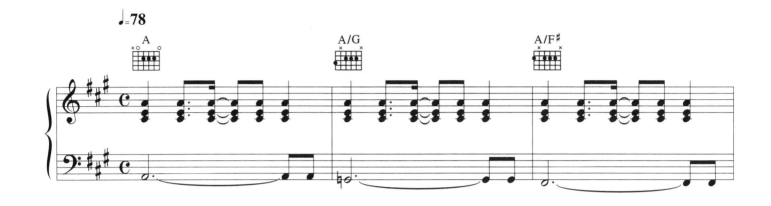

How ma-ny spe-cial peo-ple change,—

how ma-ny lives are liv-ing strange,— where were you— while we were get-ting high,—

How ma-ny spe-cial peo-ple change— how ma-ny lives are liv-ing strange,—

Verse 2:
How many special people change
How many lives are living strange
Where were you while we were getting high?
Slowly walking down the hall
Faster than a cannon ball
Where were you while we were getting high?

CHICAGO

Words and Music by
GRAHAM NASH

Male vocal written at actual pitch.

COME TO MY WINDOW

Words and Music by
MELISSA ETHERIDGE

DARK HOLLOW

Words and Music by
BILL BROWNING

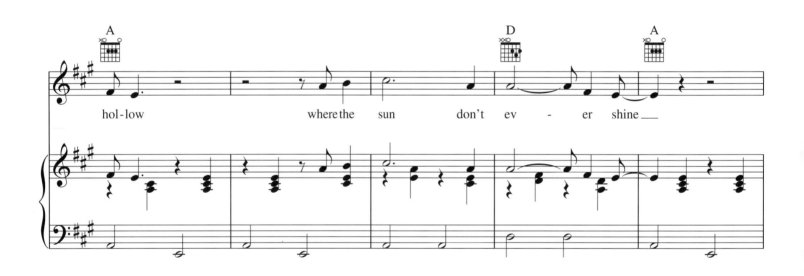

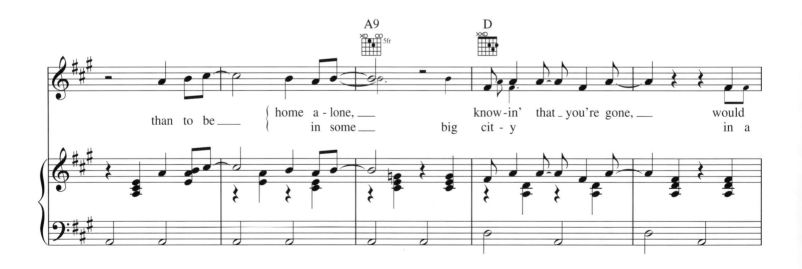

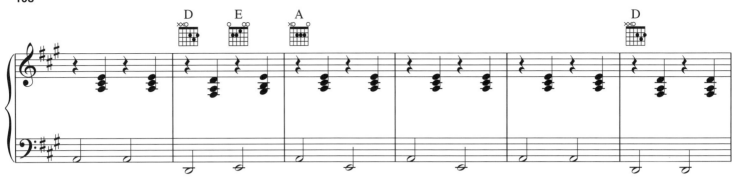

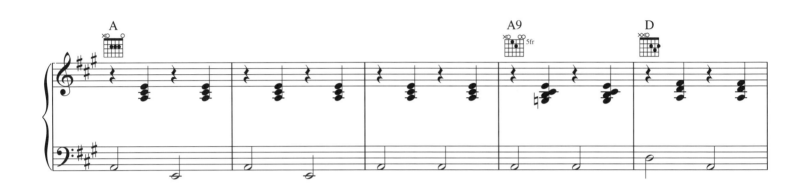

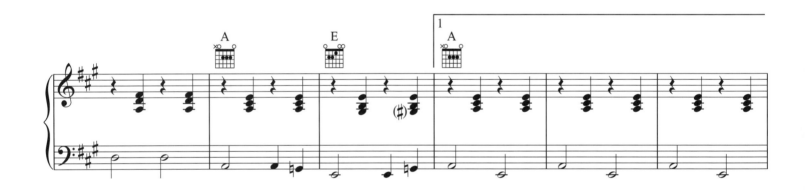

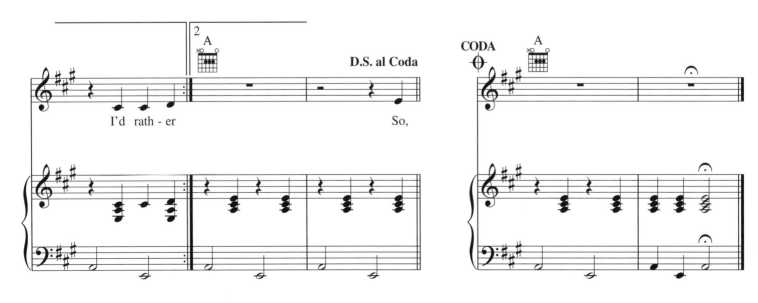

I'd rath-er

So,

THE FLAME

Words and Music by BOB MITCHELL
and NICK GRAHAM

D.S. al Coda

DONNA

Words and Music by
RITCHIE VALENS

EVERY ROSE HAS ITS THORN

Words and Music by BOBBY DALL, BRETT MICHAELS,
BRUCE JOHANNESSON and RIKKI ROCKETT

FREE FALLIN'

Words and Music by TOM PETTY
and JEFF LYNNE

She's a good girl; __ loves her ma-ma, loves

Je - sus, __ and A-mer-i-ca too. __ She's a good girl, __

cra - zy 'bout __ El - vis; loves hors - es __ and her boy-friend too.

GIVE A LITTLE BIT

Words and Music by RICK DAVIES
and ROGER HODGSON

HOLE HEARTED

Words and Music by NUNO BETTENCOURT
and GARY CHERONE

Moderate Rock

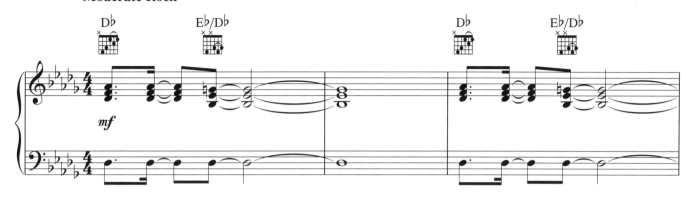

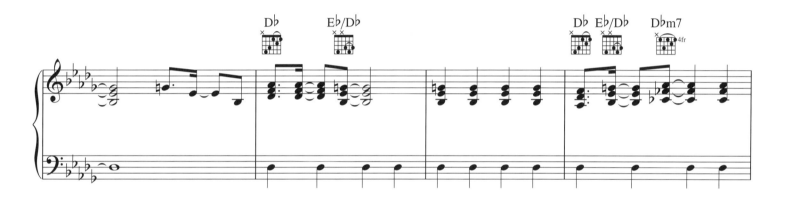

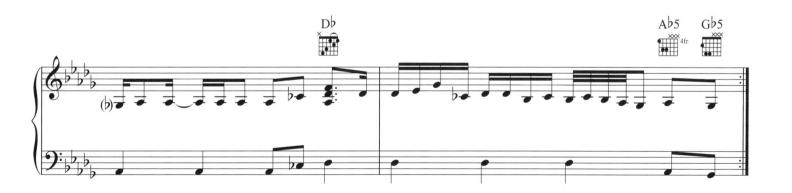

HEAVEN

Words and Music by BRYAN ADAMS
and JIM VALLANCE

HEY JUDE

Words and Music by JOHN LENNON
and PAUL McCARTNEY

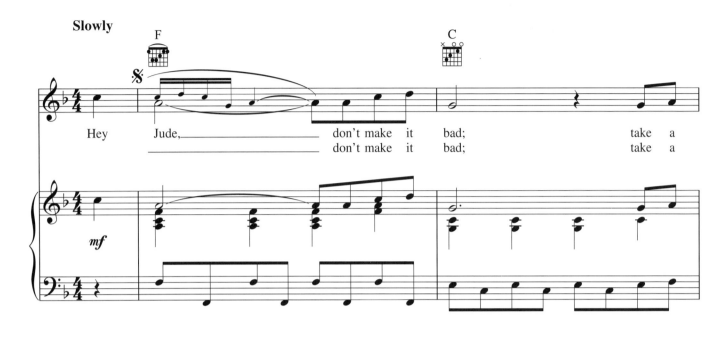

Hey Jude, don't make it bad; take a
don't make it bad; take a

sad song and make it bet - ter. Re -
sad song and make it bet - ter. Re -

mem - ber to let her in - to your heart; then you can start
mem - ber to let her un - der your skin, then you be - gin

I WANT TO KNOW WHAT LOVE IS

Words and Music by
MICK JONES

I'LL FOLLOW THE SUN

Words and Music by JOHN LENNON
and PAUL McCARTNEY

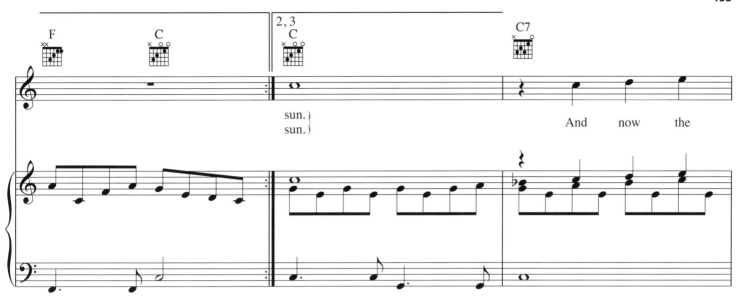

sun. }
sun. }
    And now the

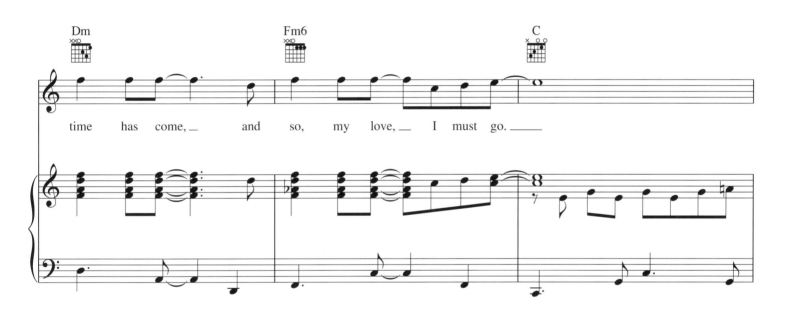

time has come, ___ and so, my love, ___ I must go. _____

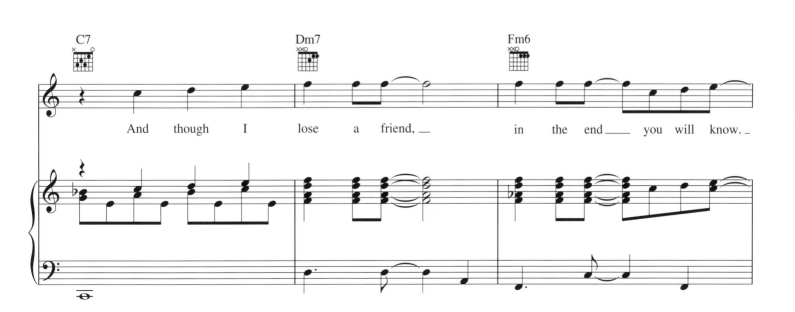

And though I lose a friend, ___ in the end ___ you will know. _

Oh, _____ one day _____
you'll find _____ that I have gone, _____ but, to-
mor - row may rain, _____ so _____ I'll fol - low the sun. _____

D.S. al Coda
(take 2nd ending)

CODA

sun. _____

IT'S A HEARTACHE

Words and Music by RONNIE SCOTT
and STEVE WOLFE

IF

Words and Music by
DAVID GATES

Moderately, with feeling

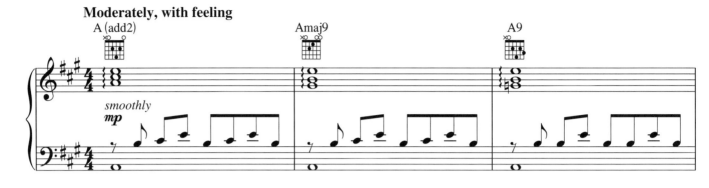

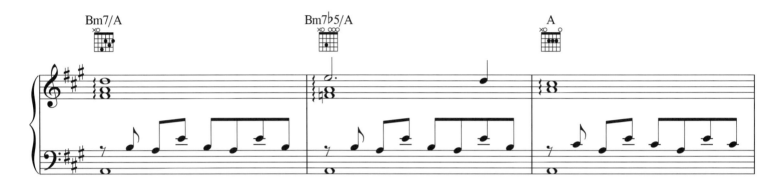

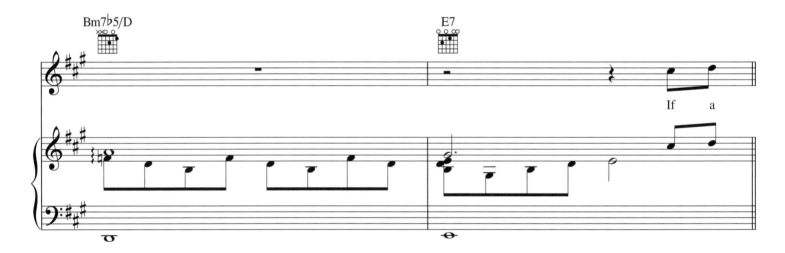

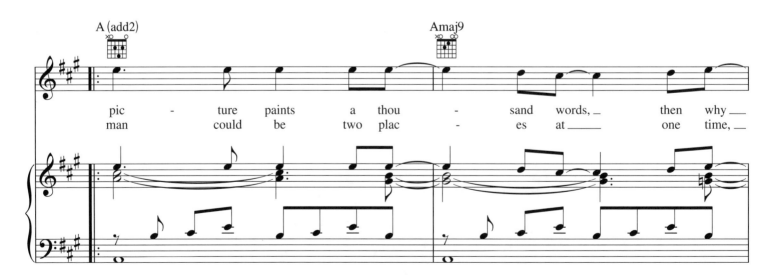

pic - ture paints a thou - sand words, ___ then why ___
man could be two plac - es at ___ one time, ___

IF I FELL

Words and Music by JOHN LENNON
and PAUL McCARTNEY

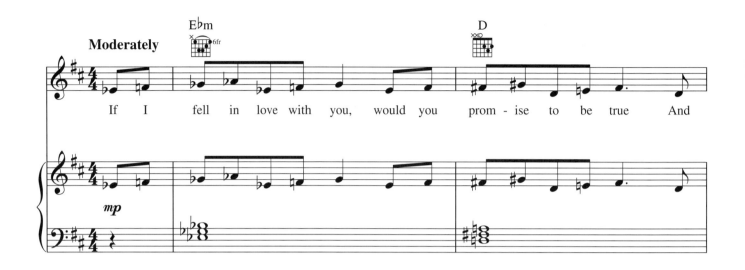

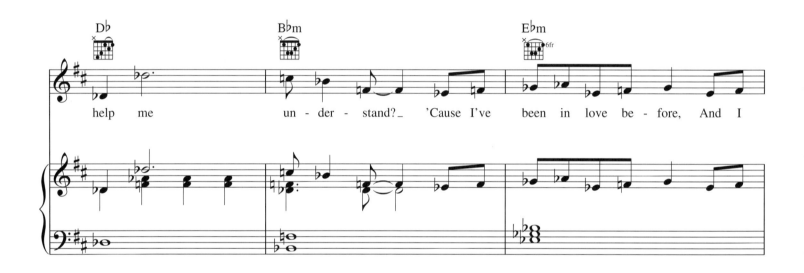

cry   when she learns we are two. _____   'Cause I

she learns we are two. _____   If I fell in love with

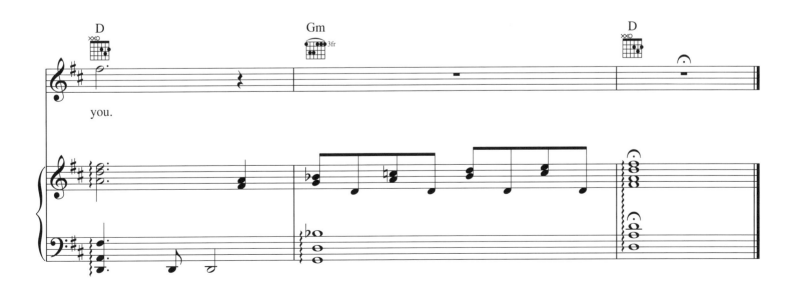

you.

IF I HAD A HAMMER

(The Hammer Song)

Words and Music by LEE HAYS
and PETE SEEGER

JACK AND DIANE

Words and Music by
JOHN MELLENCAMP

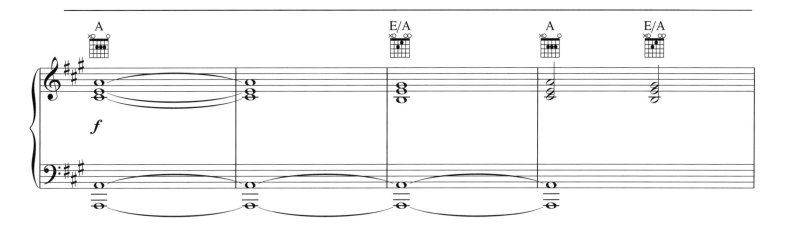

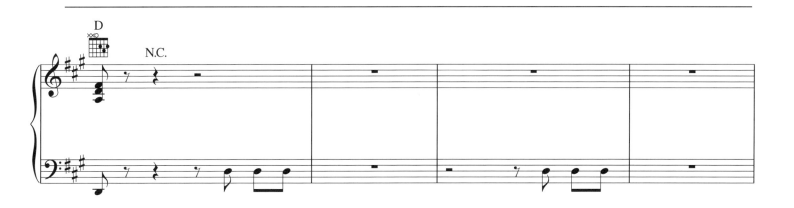

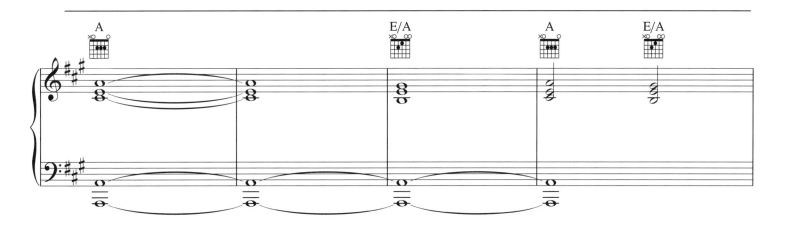

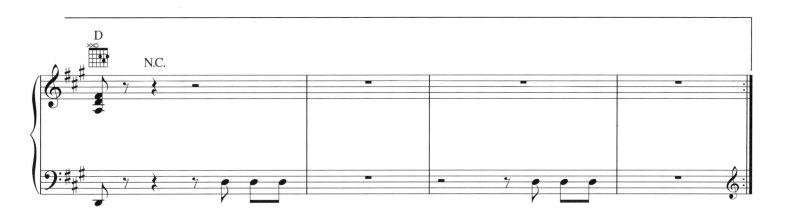

LAST NIGHT I HAD THE STRANGEST DREAM

Words and Music by
ED McCURDY

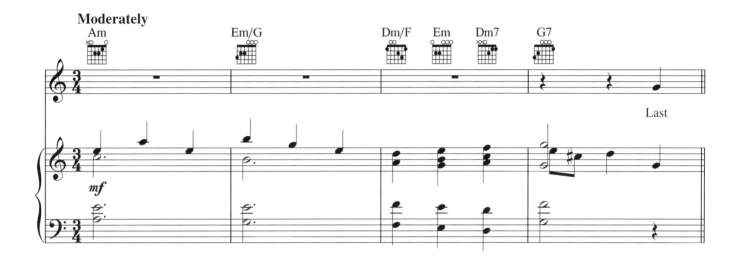

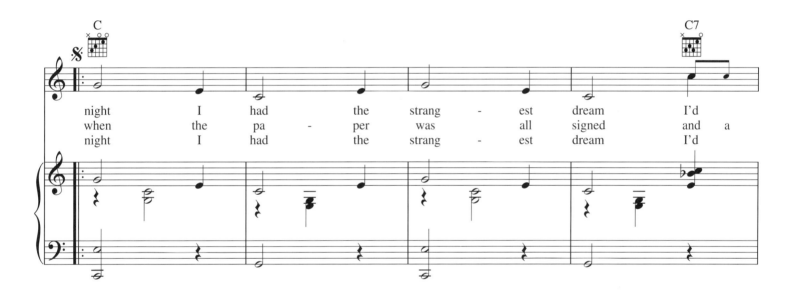

night   I   had   the   strang - est   dream   I'd
when the   pa - per   was   all   signed   and a
night   I   had   the   strang - est   dream   I'd

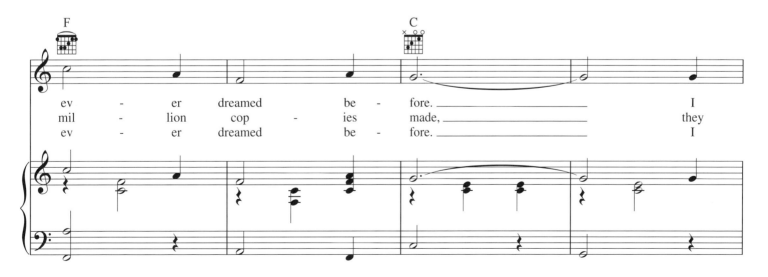

ev - er   dreamed   be - fore. _____   I
mil - lion   cop - ies   made, _____   they
ev - er   dreamed   be - fore. _____   I

JESSICA

Written by DICKEY BETTS

Up tempo Country Rock

LET'S LIVE FOR TODAY

Words and Music by GUIDO CENCIARELLI,
GIULIO RAPETTI and NORMAN DAVID

(Can't Live Without Your)
LOVE AND AFFECTION

Words and Music by MARC TANNER,
MATT NELSON and GUNNAR NELSON

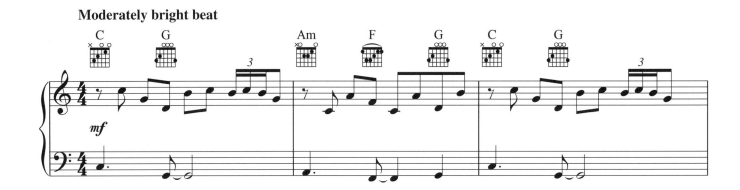

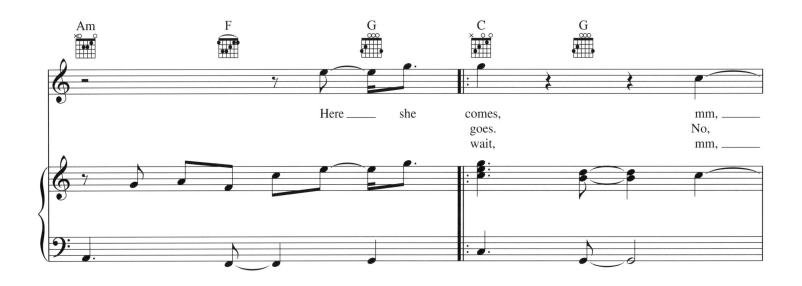

Here ___ she comes, mm, ___
goes. No,
wait, mm, ___

___ just like an an-gel. ___ Seems like for-ev-er that she's
she don't know what she's miss-ing. Can't ___ she see I'll nev-er
___ here for an an-swer. ___ Won-der if to-mor-row will be

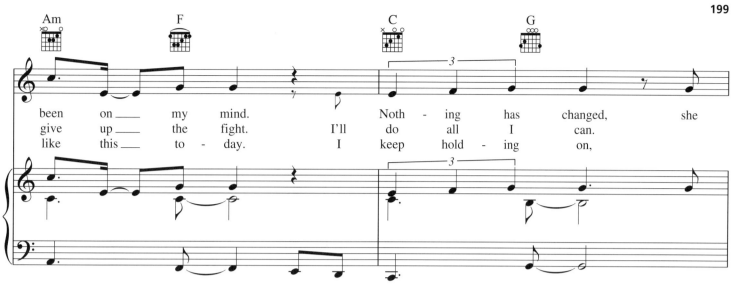

been on ____ my mind. Noth - ing has changed, she
give up ____ the fight. I'll do all I can.
like this ____ to - day. I keep hold - ing on,

thinks I'm a waste of her time. _____ There __ she
She un - der - stands my de -
can't go on liv - ing this

sire. _____ I've been on the out -
way, _____ ba - by. _____ I've been on the out -

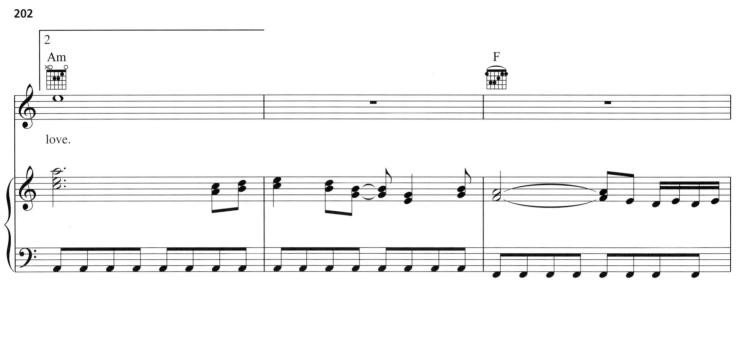

love.

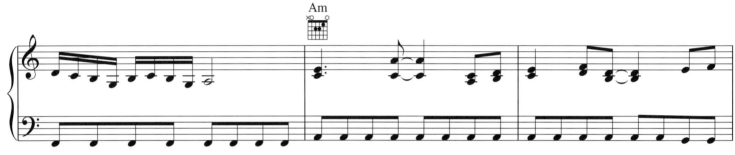

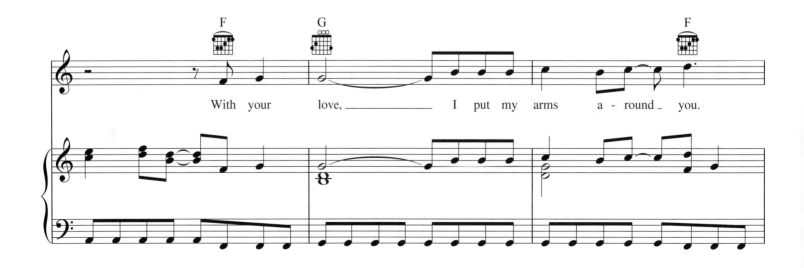

With your love, _____ I put my arms a - round _ you.

LOVE OF A LIFETIME

Words and Music by BILL LEVERTY
and CARL SNARE

I guess the time ___ was right ___ for us ___ to say ___
make a wish ___ and send it on ___ a prayer. ___

___ we'd take our time ___ and live our lives ___ to - geth -
We know our dreams ___ can all come true ___ with

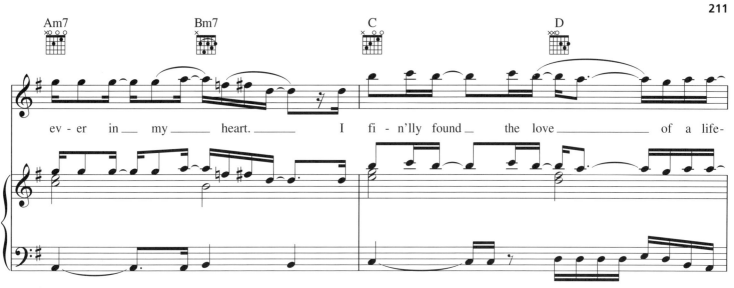

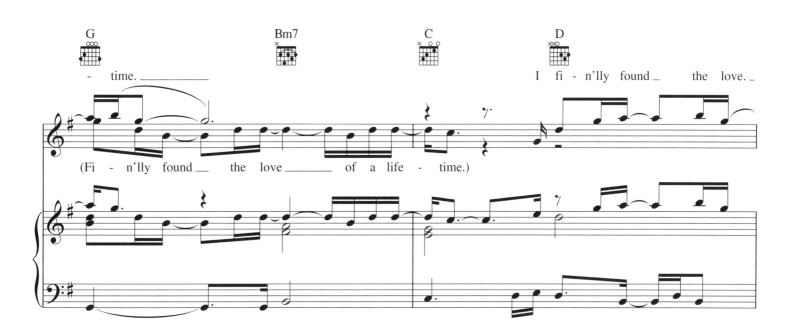

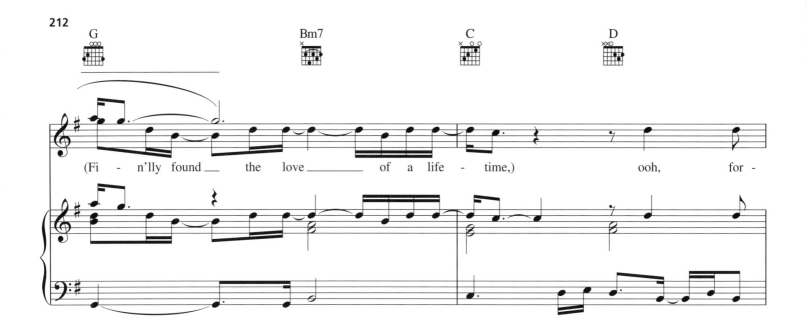

(Fi - n'lly found ___ the love ___ of a life - time,) ___ ooh, for -

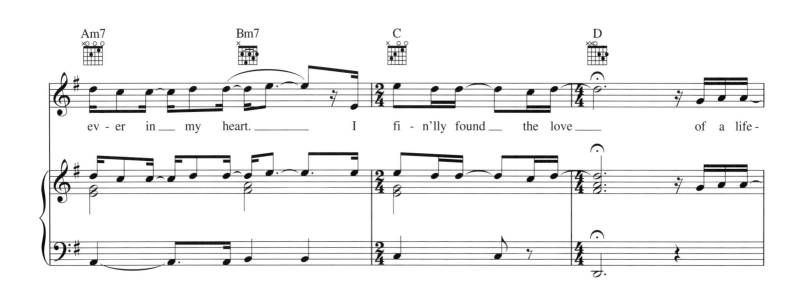

ev - er in ___ my heart. ___ I fi - n'lly found ___ the love ___ of a life -

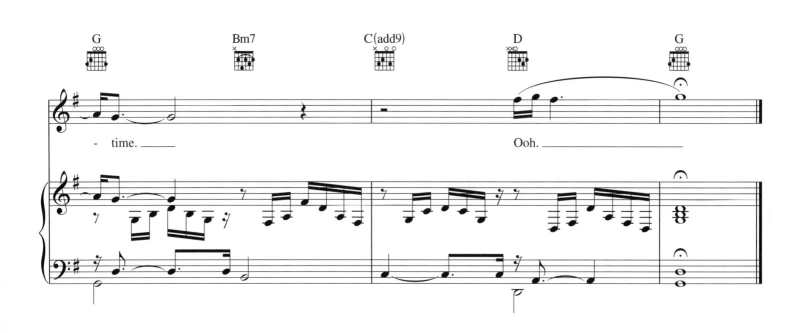

- time. ___ Ooh. ___

THE MAGIC BUS

Words and Music by
PETER TOWNSHEND

LOVER, YOU SHOULD'VE COME OVER

Words and Music by
JEFF BUCKLEY

run. ___ Some-times a man gets car-ried a - way ___ when he

feels ___ like he should be hav-ing his fun. And he's

much ___ too blind to see the dam-age he's done 'cause

some - times a man must a - wake to find that real-ly he has

MOTHER NATURE'S SON

Words and Music by JOHN LENNON
and PAUL McCARTNEY

MY SWEET LADY

Words and Music by
JOHN DENVER

NEW KID IN TOWN

Words and Music by JOHN DAVID SOUTHER,
DON HENLEY and GLENN FREY

NIGHTS IN WHITE SATIN

Words and Music by
JUSTIN HAYWARD

NOT FADE AWAY

Words and Music by CHARLES HARDIN
and NORMAN PETTY

NOTHING ELSE MATTERS

Words and Music by JAMES HETFIELD
and LARS ULRICH

*Substitute small notes 2nd time.

OPERATOR
(That's Not the Way It Feels)

Words and Music by
JIM CROCE

Op - er - a - tor, could you
Op - er - a - tor, could you
Op - er - a - tor, let's for -

help me place __ this call? __
help me place __ this call, __
get a - bout __ this call; __

You see the num - ber on the
'cause I can't read the num - ber
there's no one there I real - ly

I've learned to take it well.___ I on-ly wish my words___ could just con-vince my-self___

___ that it just was-n't real,_____ but that's not the way it feels.

PLEASE COME TO BOSTON

Words and Music by
DAVE LOGGINS

Lyrics:

He said please come to Bos - ton for __ the spring - time.
please come to Den - ver with __ the snow -
please come to L. A. __ to live __ for - ev -

- time. I'm stay - ing here __ with some friends __
- fall. We'll move up in - to the moun -
- er. A Cal - i - for - nia life __

RUN AROUND

Words and Music by
JOHN POPPER

Harmonica solo ad lib.

Oh, ___

SAY YOU LOVE ME

Words and Music by
CHRISTINE McVIE

SCARBOROUGH FAIR

Arrangement and original counter melody by
PAUL SIMON and ARTHUR GARFUNKEL

SEVEN BRIDGES ROAD

Words and Music by
STEPHEN T. YOUNG

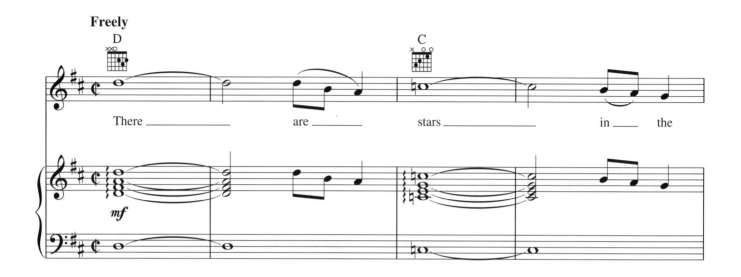

There _____ are _____ stars _____ in ___ the

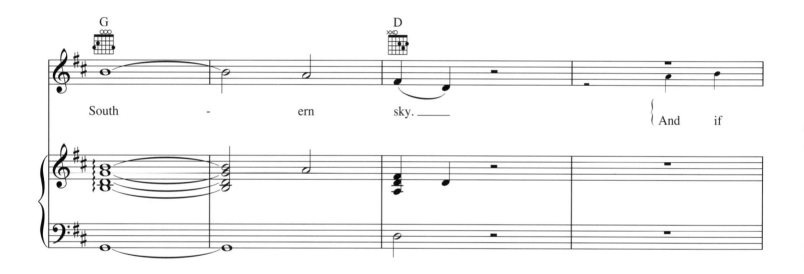

South - ern sky. _____ And if

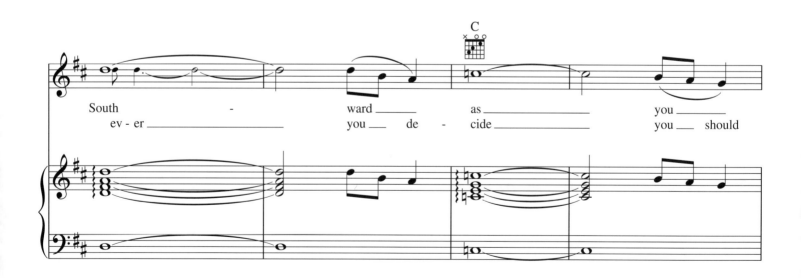

South - ward _____ as _____ you _____
ev - er _____ you de - cide _____ you __ should

Bright Country

SIGNS

Words and Music by
LES EMMERSON

SOMEBODY TO LOVE

Words and Music by
DARBY SLICK

When the truth is found __ to be __

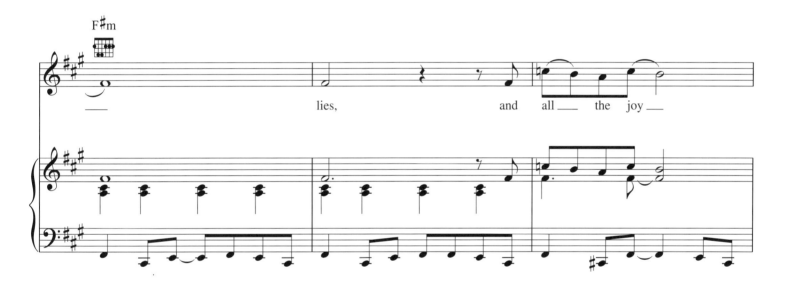

__ lies, and all __ the joy __

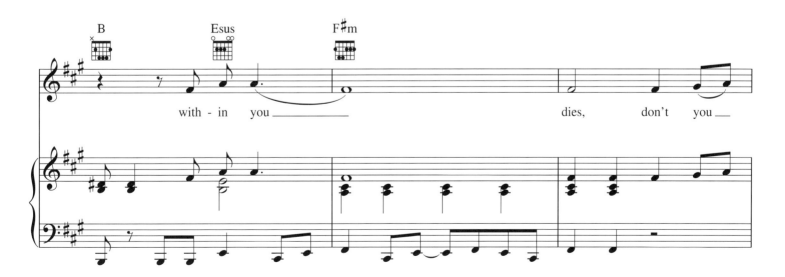

with - in you __ dies, don't you __

SOAK UP THE SUN

Words and Music by JEFF TROTT
and SHERYL CROW

STARMAN

Words and Music by
DAVID BOWIE

SUITE: JUDY BLUE EYES

Words and Music by
STEPHEN STILLS

Chest-nut - brown _ ca - nar - y, _____ ru - by - throat - ed spar -
Voic - es of _____ the an - gels, _____ ring a - round _ the moon -
Lac - y, lilt - ing lyr - ic, _____ los - ing love, _ la - ment -

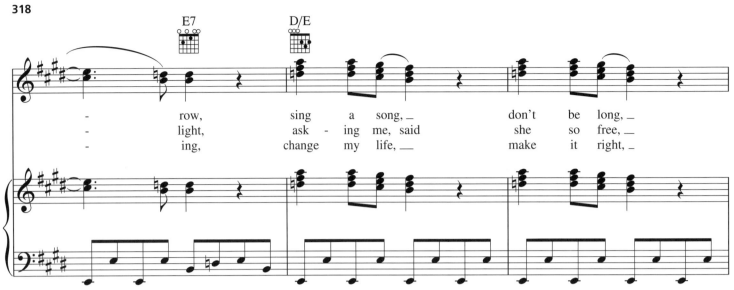

Do do do do do, do   do   do do do do,   do do do do do,   do   do do do.

SUNSHINE ON MY SHOULDERS

Words by JOHN DENVER
Music by JOHN DENVER, MIKE TAYLOR and DICK KNISS

TANGLED UP IN BLUE

Words and Music by
BOB DYLAN

1. Ear - ly one morn - in' the sun __ was shin - in', I was lay - in' in bed, __
2. She __ was mar - ried when we __ first met, soon to be __ di - vorced. __
3. I had a job in the great __ North woods, work - in' as a cook for a spell. __ But I

4.-7. *(See additional lyrics)*
8. *Instrumental*

won - d'rin' if __ she's changed at all, __ if her hair was __ still red. __
I helped her out of a jam, I guess, __ but I used a lit - tle too much force. __
nev - er did like __ it all that much __ and one day the axe just fell. __ So I

We

326

Tan - gled up in blue. ___
tan - gled up in blue. ___

Additional Lyrics

4. She was working in topless place
   And I stopped in for a beer.
   I just kept looking at the side of her face
   In the spotlight so clear.
   And later on when the crowd thinned out
   I was just about to do the same.
   She was standing there in back of my chair,
   Said to me, "Don't I know your name?"
   I muttered something underneath my breath.
   She studied the lines on my face.
   I must admit I felt a little uneasy
   When she bent down to tie the laces of my shoe,
   Tangled up in blue.

5. She lit a burner on the stove
   And offered me a pipe.
   "I thought you'd never say hello," she said.
   "You look like the silent type."
   Then she opened up a book of poems
   And handed it to me,
   Written by an Italian poet
   From the thirteenth century.
   And every one of them words rang true
   And glowed like burning coal,
   Pourin' off of every page
   Like it was written in my soul,
   From me to you,
   Tangled up in blue.

6. I lived with them on Montague Street
   In a basement down the stairs.
   There was music in the cafes at night
   And revolution in the air.
   Then he started in the dealing in slaves
   And something inside of him died.
   She had to sell everything she owned
   And froze up inside.
   And when finally the bottom finally fell out
   I became withdrawn.
   The only thing I knew how to do
   Was to keep on keeping on,
   Like a bird that flew
   Tangled up in blue.

7. So now I'm going back again.
   I got to get to her somehow.
   All the people we used to know,
   They're an illusion to me now.
   Some are mathematicians,
   Some are carpenter's wives.
   Don't know how it all got started,
   I don't know what they do with their lives.
   But me, I'm still on the road
   Headin' for another joint.
   We always did feel the same,
   We just saw it from a different point of view,
   Tangled up in blue.

TEACH YOUR CHILDREN

Words and Music by
GRAHAM NASH

You ... who are on the road ___

D.S. al Coda

world that we can live in.)
be - fore ___ they can ___ die. _____

CODA

love _____ you.

WE CAN WORK IT OUT

Words and Music by JOHN LENNON
and PAUL McCARTNEY

Try to see it my way, do I have to keep on talk-ing
Think of what you're say - ing, you can get it wrong and still you

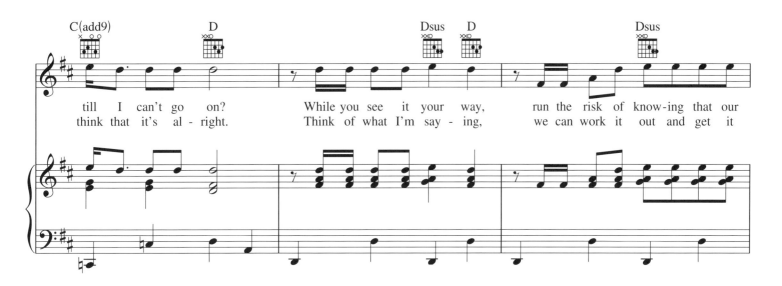

till I can't go on? While you see it your way, run the risk of know-ing that our
think that it's al - right. Think of what I'm say-ing, we can work it out and get it

love may soon be gone.)
straight, or say good - night.)   We can work it out, we can work it out. _____

THICK AS A BRICK

Words and Music by
IAN ANDERSON

Moderately, in 2

TIME FOR ME TO FLY

Words and Music by
KEVIN CRONIN

I've been a - round ____ for you, been up and down ____ for ____ you; but
You said we'd work ____ it out. You said that you had ____ no ____ doubt that

I just can't get an - y re - lief. ____ I've
deep down we were real - ly in love. ____ But

TOM DOOLEY

Words and Music Collected, Adapted and Arranged by
FRANK WARNER, JOHN A. LOMAX and ALAN LOMAX
From the singing of FRANK PROFFITT

TORN

Words and Music by PHIL THORNALLEY,
SCOTT CUTLER and ANNE PREVIN

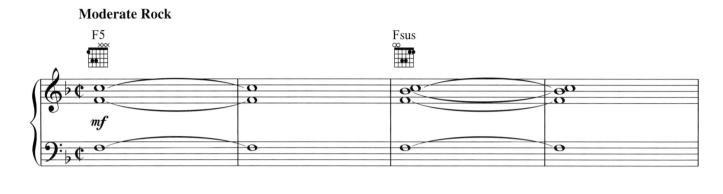

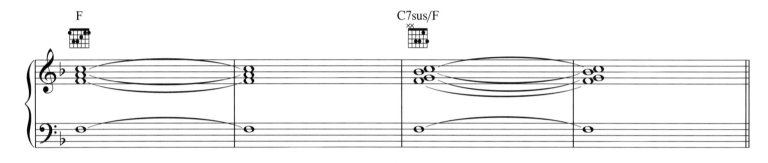

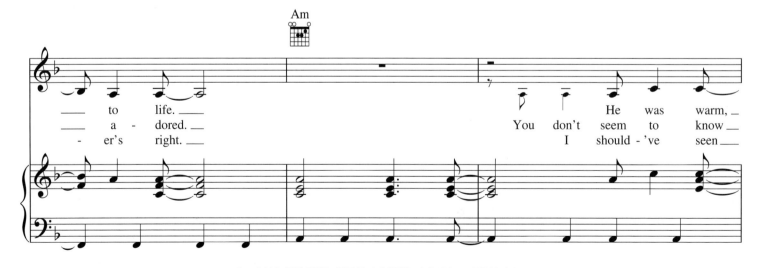

TWO OF US

Words and Music by JOHN LENNON
and PAUL McCARTNEY

Brightly, in 2

1. Two of us, rid - ing no - where, spend - ing some -
2. Two of us, send - ing post - cards, writ - ing let -
3,4. Two of us, wear - ing rain - coats, stand - ing so -

- one's hard - earned pay.
- ers, on my wall.
- lo, in the sun.

359

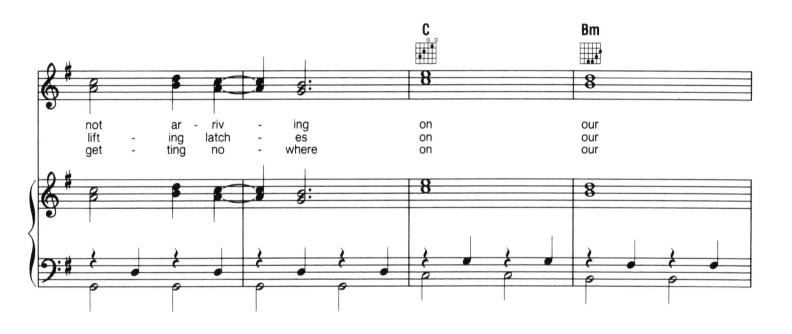

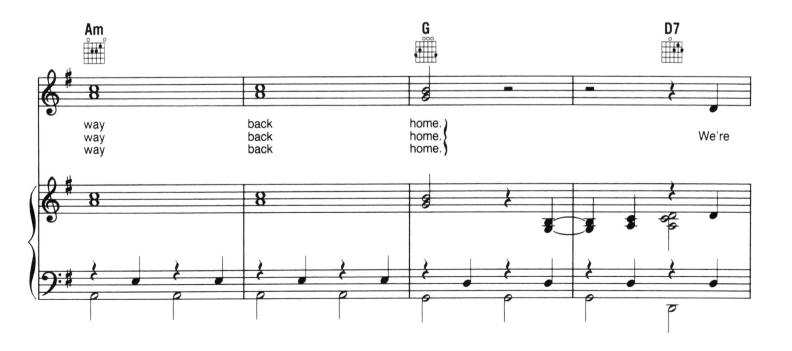

TWO OUT OF THREE AIN'T BAD

Words and Music by
JIM STEINMAN

WALK RIGHT IN

Words and Music by GUS CANNON
and H. WOODS

WANTED DEAD OR ALIVE

Words and Music by JON BON JOVI
and RICHIE SAMBORA

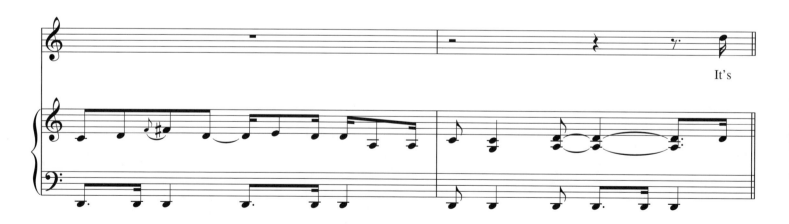

WASTED ON THE WAY

Words and Music by
GRAHAM NASH

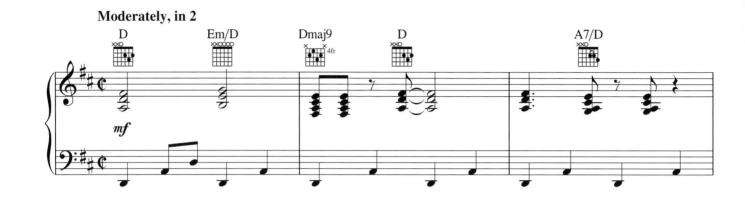

Look a - round _____ me. I can
you were young, did you

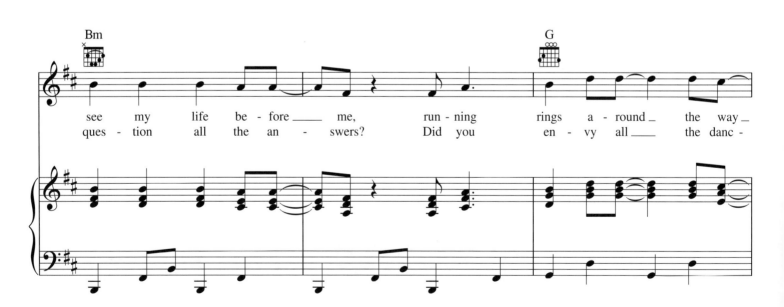

see my life be - fore _____ me, run - ning rings a - round _____ the way
ques - tion all the an - swers? Did you en - vy all _____ the danc -

WE SHALL OVERCOME

Musical and Lyrical Adaptation by ZILPHIA HORTON,
FRANK HAMILTON, GUY CARAWAN and PETE SEEGER
Inspired by African American Gospel Singing, members of the Food and Tobacco
Workers Union, Charleston, SC, and the southern Civil Rights Movement

Moderately slow, with determination

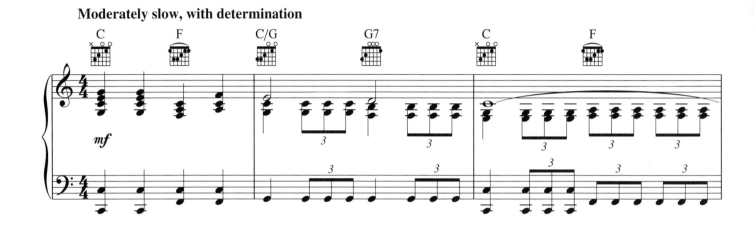

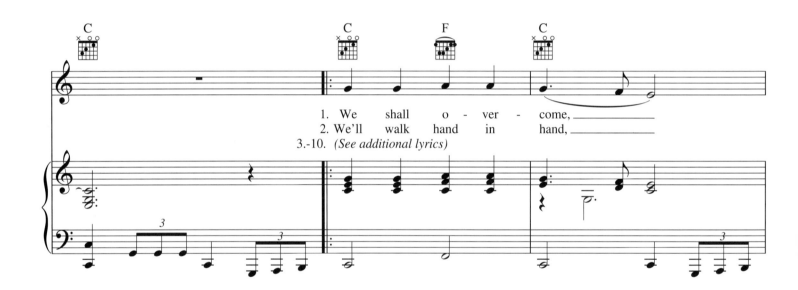

1. We shall o - ver - come, _____
2. We'll walk hand in hand, _____
3.-10. *(See additional lyrics)*

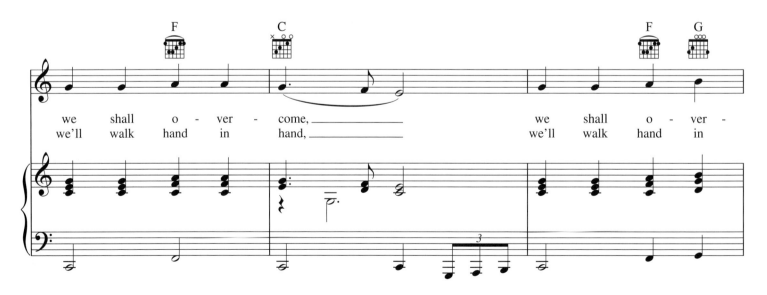

we shall o - ver - come, _____ we shall o - ver -
we'll walk hand in hand, _____ we'll walk hand in

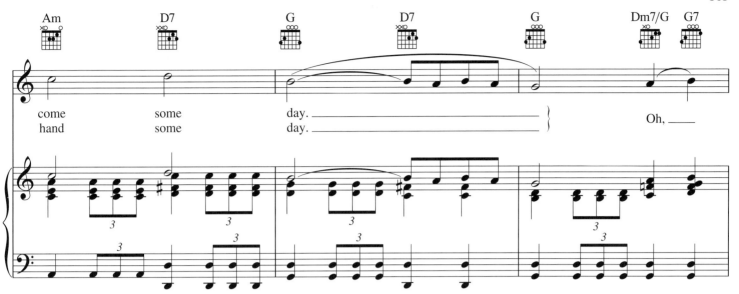

come some day. _____ Oh, _____
hand some day. _____

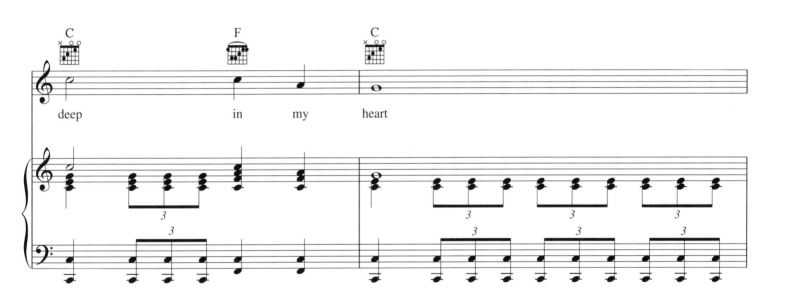

deep in my heart

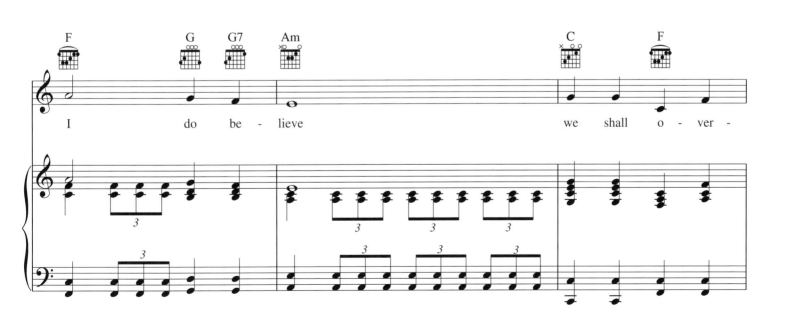

I do be - lieve we shall o - ver -

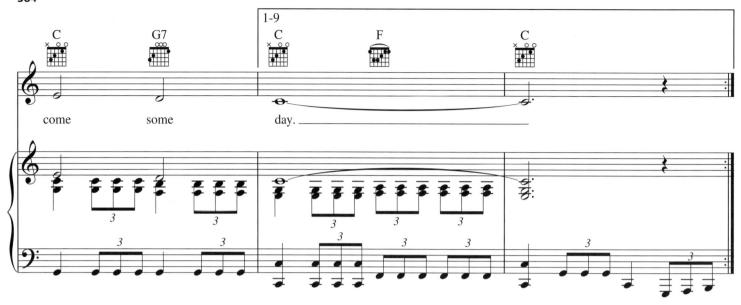

come   some   day.

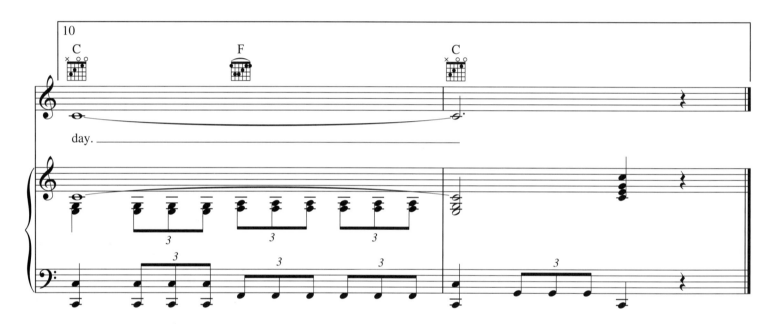

day.

Additional Lyrics

3. We are not afraid, we are not afraid,
   We are not afraid today.
   Oh, deep in my heart I do believe
   We shall overcome some day.

4. We shall stand together, we shall stand together,
   We shall stand together now.
   Oh, deep in my heart I do believe
   We shall overcome some day.

5. The truth will make us free, the truth will make us free,
   The truth will make us free some day.
   Oh, deep in my heart I do believe
   We shall overcome some day.

6. The Lord will see us through, the Lord will see us through,
   The Lord will see us through some day.
   Oh, deep in my heart I do believe
   We shall overcome some day.

7. We shall be like Him, we shall be like Him,
   We shall be like Him some day.
   Oh, deep in my heart I do believe
   We shall overcome some day.

8. We shall live in peace, we shall live in peace,
   We shall live in peace someday.
   Oh, deep in my heart I do believe
   We shall overcome some day.

9. The whole wide world around, the whole wide world around,
   The whole wide world around some day.
   Oh, deep in my heart I do believe
   We shall overcome some day.

10. We shall overcome, we shall overcome,
    We shall overcome some day.
    Oh, deep in my heart I do believe
    We shall overcome some day.

YOU WERE MEANT FOR ME

Words and Music by JEWEL KILCHER
and STEVE POLTZ

WHEN THE CHILDREN CRY

Words and Music by MIKE TRAMP
and VITO BRATTA

Em · D · C

no one knows __ just why. ____ What have
love and _____ peace. No more

Bm · Em · Bm

we be - gun? __ Just __ look what we have done. __
pres - i - dents, __ and __ all the wars will end; __

C · G · Em

All that we ____ de - stroyed __ you must build a -
one u - ni - ted world __ un - der

D · Dsus · D · Em · Bm

gain. __ }
God. __ } When the chil - dren __ cry, let them

mf

WILD WORLD

Words and Music by
CAT STEVENS

YOU'VE GOT TO HIDE YOUR LOVE AWAY

Words and Music by JOHN LENNON
and PAUL McCARTNEY

YOU'RE IN MY HEART

Words and Music by
ROD STEWART

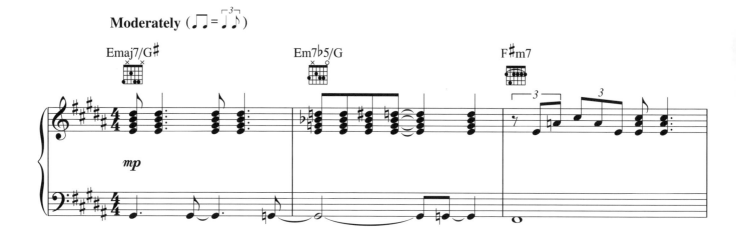

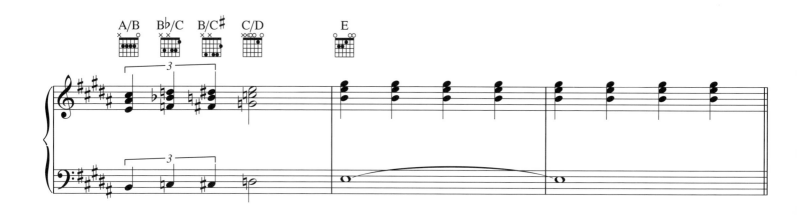

I did - n't know ___ what day it was ___ when you walked ___
I took all ___ those hab - its of yours that in the be -